Manifestation & Magic

Poetry for the Soulpreneur

Lindsay McCellon

BookLeaf Publishing

India | USA | UK

Made with ❤ on the BookLeaf Publishing Platform
www.bookleafpub.in
www.bookleafpub.com

Dedication

To my children—my greatest inspiration. You are the reason I strive to manifest a brighter, more magical life every day. May you always believe in your dreams and the power within you.

To my husband—my rock, my cheerleader, my partner in magic. Your unwavering support and love remind me that anything is possible.

To my mother—thank you for always encouraging me to embrace my weird, wild, and wonderful self. Your wisdom and love have been the spark that ignites my magic.

With love, light, and infinite gratitude.

Acknowledgement

No magic is ever written alone. This book is a manifestation of love, support, and the unwavering encouragement of the incredible souls in my life, and though I have said some of this in my dedication... some of this bears repeating:

To my children—you are my motivation, my reason for growth, and my greatest teachers. Thank you for inspiring me to create a life rich in purpose and magic.

To my husband—your unwavering belief in me has been my greatest source of strength. You have always supported my wildest dreams, and for that, I am eternally grateful.

To my mother—thank you for teaching me to embrace my uniqueness. Your encouragement to be my weird, magical self has given me the confidence to walk this path with authenticity and courage.

To Sara Bettale—my bestie, my soul sister, my inspiration. Your fearless pursuit of your own soul's calling has shown me what is possible. Thank you for always reminding me to honor my own journey and build a business rooted in passion and purpose.

To my book editor and publisher—thank you for creating a process that felt not just achievable but enjoyable. You made this journey feel aligned and accessible, and for that, I am deeply grateful.

To the mentors from my corporate career—whether you realized it or not, you helped me discover my voice. Your guidance shaped the way I express myself and step into my power.

To my friends and soul family—thank you for your encouragement, for holding space for my dreams, and for always cheering me on. Your belief in me has meant the world.

To my readers—this book is for you. Whether you are a creator, a soulpreneur, a modern witch, or simply someone seeking more magic in life, I hope these words inspire and empower you.

And finally, to the Universe—thank you for the signs, the synchronicities, the challenges, and the lessons. This book is proof of the magic that unfolds when you follow the quiet pull of your soul's calling.

With infinite gratitude,
Lindsay McCellon

Preface

This book is a spellbook in verse—a collection of poetry woven with intention, manifestation, and the journey of the soulpreneur. It is for the dreamers who dare to turn passion into purpose, for the witches who craft their own destiny, and for the creators who infuse their work with magic.

For years, I searched for alignment, for a way to merge my spirituality, creativity, and ambition. I found my answers in Tarot cards, in crochet, in modern witchcraft, and in the realization that business can be a sacred practice. This book is the embodiment of that journey—each poem a window into a life of manifestation.

May these words inspire you to trust your path, embrace your unique magic, and create a life that feels truly aligned with your soul.

With love and enchantment,
Lindsay

The Spark

A whisper soft, a glowing light,
A flicker dancing in the night.
A tiny ember, warm and bright—
A spark is born; it takes to flight.

It hums inside, it starts to grow,
A secret only dreamers know.
It twirls, it spins, it lights the way,
A quiet voice that dares to stay.

"You hold the magic," says the flame,
"A soul's desire—just call its name!"
With open hands, you fan it high,
A wish... a word... a battle cry.

The world may hush, the doubt may creep,
But sparks aren't meant to fall asleep.
So feed the fire, let it rise,
A star is burning in your eyes.

For dreams begin where sparks ignite,
A tiny glow—a blazing light.
And all it takes to start anew,
Is knowing that the spark is you.

Trust the Pull

A whisper calls, so soft, so sweet,
Like ocean waves that kiss your feet.
A tug, a nudge, a fleeting glow,
A secret only dreamers know.

It pulls you left, it pulls you right,
It sings beneath the pale moonlight.
It weaves through dreams and lingers near,
A voice that only you can hear.

At times it's wild, at times it's still,
A compass forged of heart and will.
It bends, it sways, it shifts, it swirls,
A thread that binds you to the world.

But fear will whisper, "Not today."
It tries to steal the spark away.
Yet deep inside, you've always known—
The path is yours, and yours alone.

So trust the pull, embrace the flight,
Step through the dark and find the light.
For magic waits, but makes no sound—
It only stirs where faith is found.

The Fool's First Step

A foot poised high, a breath drawn deep,
A path ahead, a chance to leap.
The world behind, the stars above,
A journey etched with trust and love.

The cliff is steep, the way is new,
But fate is calling—will you answer too?
The sun is bright, the breeze is kind,
A voice that whispers, "Trust your mind."

The road is wild, the road is free,
It bends, it twists—a mystery!
Yet still, you step with heart so light,
For faith can turn the dark to bright.

Some say you're lost, some say you're blind,
But dreams aren't made by those confined.
So laugh, so leap, so dare to try—
The Fool will teach you how to fly.

Messages in the Cards

Shuffle once and shuffle twice,
Lay them down and roll the dice.
Whispers hum, the candles glow,
The cards reveal what spirits know.

A Queen, a Fool, a Tower tall,
The rise, the fall, the fate of all.
A Wheel that spins, a Moon so bright,
A Star that shimmers in the night.

Some will warn and some will guide,
Some reveal what hides inside.
Each one speaks—a thread, a clue,
A voice that says, "This path is you."

But heed them not with fear or woe,
For all they show is what you know.
The truth was always in your hands—
The cards just help you understand.

Dream it into Being

Close your eyes and paint the scene,
A world that shimmers, gilded green.
Feel the joy, embrace the glow,
See it, taste it—make it so.

Speak the words, the spell is cast,
The future bends, release the past.
Write it down, declare the way,
The dream you hold begins today.

The stars take note, the winds will shift,
The universe wraps up your gift.
But faith must burn, your heart must trust,
For dreams take root in fearless dust.

Doubt may whisper, "Not so fast,"
Fear will haunt you, make you ask—
But magic answers those who dare,
So step ahead—the path is there.

For what you dream is what you weave,
A world that breathes because you believe.

The Tower Falls

The sky is cracking, lightning screams,
It shatters walls and shreds your dreams.
The ground below begins to shake,
The life you knew starts to break.

The tower falls—stone by stone,
Leaving you lost, afraid, and alone.
But in the dust, the truth is bright:
The fire burns to bring new light.

For towers built on fear and lies
Will crumble so the soul can rise.
What once was safe may hold you back,
What once felt firm may start to crack.

But do not fear the fall, my dear,
For after flames, the air is clear.
And in the rubble, soft and true,
A path appears—designed for you.

Alchemy of the Soul

A spark, a flame, a fire bright,
A dance between the dark and light.
The things that broke, the scars that stayed,
Are golden within the art you've made.

The tears once spilled, the nights once long,
Now hum inside—a battle song.
The doubt, the loss, the twist of fate,
Were embers in the hands of greats.

For alchemy is more than gold,
It's how we shine from pain we hold.
It's how we turn the wounds so deep
Into a strength that we can keep.

So forge your past in fire's embrace,
Let every trial carve its place.
For magic isn't just the new—
It's built from all that you've been through.

The Empress Creates

She walks where wild roses bloom,
A crown of stars, a heart in tune.
Her hands hold soil, fertile and deep,
She plants the dreams the soul must keep.

With golden touch, she weaves, she spins,
She births new worlds where life begins.
A whisper soft, a seed so small,
Yet soon it grows beyond the wall.

She paints, she writes, she shapes, she sings,
She conjures life in endless things.
For what she dreams, she dares to do—
And all she touches turns brand new.

The Empress knows: to give, to grow,
To love, to trust, to let it flow.
Abundance shines from those who share,
And magic lives in hands that care

Hanged Between Doubt & Trust

I dangle here, the world is still,
No need to chase, no fight, no will.
The tides will turn, the winds will shift,
For patience is a sacred gift.

The mind will beg, "Go find the way!"
But wisdom whispers, "Wait. Obey."
For answers come when rushings cease,
And clarity is born from peace.

The world looks strange from upside-down,
The fears dissolve, the thoughts unbound.
What once seemed lost now glows so bright—
For trust reveals the hidden light.

And so I sway, and so I learn,
That time will bring the path in turn.
No force, no fear - just let it be,
What's meant for me will come to me.

Wheel of Fortune

Round and round, the wheel will turn,
Lessons given, lessons learned.
Highs and lows, the fate we chase,
Yet every shift at divine pace.

The climb is sweet, the fall is steep,
Yet both are gifts the soul must keep.
For even storms will clear the skies,
And even loss brings a new sunrise.

No moment lasts, no fate is set,
The tides will rise, the tides will rest.
For luck is not in hands we hold,
But placed in faith... to dance when told.

So spin the wheel and trust its song,
No place you land is ever wrong.
For every turn, both fast and slow,
Will bring you where you're meant to go.

The Sacred Stitch

A loop, a pull, a twist, a turn,
The hands create, the fingers learn.
A single thread, so soft, so tight,
Becomes a weave of dark and light.

Each stitch a wish, each row a prayer,
A whispered spell spun through the air.
The pattern builds, the knots align,
A dance of patience, pure, divine.

Some threads tangle, some may fray,
Yet hands will guide them back in play.
For every loop, both old and new,
Holds love, holds hope, holds something true.

So weave your magic, soft and strong,
And hum your spell as you go along.
For stitched in fiber, row by row,
Are dreams that only you bestow.

Words as Spells

A whisper soft, a voice so bright,
A spell is cast in spoken light.
A wish, a vow, a dream unsaid,
Becomes alive when boldly led.

The words we speak, the words we weave,
Are threads of fate—so speak, believe.
For every phrase, both kind and true,
Can shape the world surrounding you.

Say "I am strong," and strength will rise,
Say "I am free," and watch it fly.
Say "I am worthy," stand up tall—
Your words will lift you through it all.

But words can break and words can bind,
So use them well, be clear, be kind.
For what you say, you bring to be—
So weave your spells intentionally.

Light the Candle, Set the Spell

A wick stands tall, the match strikes bright,
A flicker dances into light.
The air grows thick, the whispers hum,
The magic starts—the spell's begun.

A breath so deep, a wish so true,
The flame will know just what to do.
It sways, it bends, it leaps, it glows,
A secret only fire knows.

With every word, the embers gleam,
They hold your hopes, they shape your dream.
For flames will carry, swift and fast,
The future forming from the past.

So light the candle, set it free,
And trust in what is meant to be.
For what you seek is seeking you,
And fire makes the old brand new.

Manifestation Moon

The new moon whispers, soft and low,
A seed to plant, a wish to grow.
I close my eyes, my heart takes flight,
A dream is born in silver light.

The crescent hums, a spark, a start,
A quiet pull inside my heart.
The first step calls, the path is clear,
I walk in faith, release my fear.

The full moon shines, so big, so bold,
A story written bright in gold.
The wish I spoke, the spell I wove,
Now blooms beneath its lunar glow.

And as it wanes, I let things rest,
Releasing all that serves me less.
For every phase, both fast and slow,
Will bring the life I've dared to grow.

Cauldron of Ideas

A spark, a thought, a whisper bright,
A flicker glowing in the night.
I stir the dream, I watch it rise,
A vision forming in my eyes.

A pinch of hope, a dash of dare,
A drop of faith hangs in the air.
A swirl of ink, a stitch, a rhyme,
A spell of art, a dance in time.

It bubbles, brews, it starts to glow,
A rush of magic starts to flow.
For what we dream and dare to do,
Becomes the life we're stepping to.

So stir your thoughts, let fire ignite,
Breathe in the muse, create in light.
For all you seek, both bold and true,
Begins first as a spark in you.

Money is Energy

Coins will jingle, bills will fold,
Money flows like rivers of gold.
Not just paper, not just trade,
But energy in form we've made.

Give with joy and watch it grow,
What you send will surely flow.
Hold it tight, it turns to dust,
Abundance blooms through faith and trust.

It's not the chase, it's not the hoard,
But knowing you are always stored.
For wealth is not just in your hands,
But in your heart, your dreams, your plans.

So spend with love and earn with grace,
Know fortune holds an open space.
For money moves like air, like sea—
And all you give returns to thee.

Selling is Sacred

A gift, a craft, a spark inside,
A light too bright to run or hide.
You wove it pure, you built it true,
A piece of magic born of you.

To share, to serve, to let it shine,
To place it in another's time.
Not begging, chasing, feeling small,
But knowing it was meant for all.

For selling is a sacred thread,
A spell that leaves your hands, then spreads.
A giving, taking, fair exchange,
A shift, a dance, a life arranged.

So ask with love, receive with grace,
Let wealth and worth both hold their place.
For what you give and what you share,
Brings ripples far beyond your care.

Boundaries are Spells

A whispered no, a line drawn clear,
A shield of love, a stance sincere.
No need to fight, no need to shout,
A spell is cast—what's in stays out.

My time, my space, my sacred ground,
Not all may step where I am found.
For energy is gold so rare,
And I must choose with love and care.

A wall of peace, a door of grace,
Not built in fear, but held in place.
For those who knock with love, I see,
But not all hands may turn my key.

So call it firm, or call it kind,
But know my power stays mine.
For every "no" I dare to weave,
Creates the space where I can breathe.

The Ghost

It lingers soft, it whispers low,
A shadow creeping where I go.
"You're not enough," it sighs, it sneers,
A voice I've carried through the years.

It haunts my work, it dims my fire,
It pulls me back into the quagmire.
Yet when I turn to meet its gaze,
I see—it's only fear in haze.

For ghosts aren't real, they hold no shape,
They fade like mist at dawn's escape.
And doubt is just a fleeting mist,
That vanishes when I persist.

So I will write, create, be bold,
Step forth in light, let dreams unfold.
For ghosts may whisper, haunt, and groan,
But power only lies in bone.

Co-Creation

A single spark, a whispered dream,
A thread that shimmers, gold and gleam.
But hands unseen will weave and spin,
The universe is listening.

I take a step, the stars align,
A hidden rhythm beats with mine.
For every wish, for every call,
The universe is there through it all.

I shape, I mold, I cast, I invoke,
Yet fate still waltzes through the flow.
Not mine alone, not chance or scheme,
But co-creation, light, and dream.

So I will trust, release, allow,
Let magic meet me in the now.
For what I build, both bright and true,
The universe is growing too.

I Am the Magic

No wand to wave, no spell to cast,
No fate is written, set, or past.
No whispered wish, no secret key,
The magic has always been me.

I shape, I build, I dream, I weave,
I call, I claim, I dare, believe.
For what I seek, I first must be,
The power lives inside of me.

No stars decide, no winds command,
No force but mine will shape my hand.
The path, the spark, the light I crave—
All rise within—they do not wave.

So here I stand, both fierce and free,
No longer waiting—I decree!
For every dream, both wild and new,
Is born the moment I choose to.

The Road: A Winding Spell

The road calls out, a whispered name,
A trail of stars, a path of flame.
With every step, the old unbinds,
The past dissolves, the soul unwinds.

The wheels will turn, the world will bend,
A journey starts but has no end.
Each mile a chant, each stop a sign,
A sacred map, a fate divine.

For those who wander, those who roam,
Each place they touch becomes a home.
And with the wind, the heart will swell—
For every road casts its own spell.

Feet on Earth, Head in the Stars

Barefoot steps on sacred ground,
Yet dreams still call without a sound.
The earth is firm beneath my stride,
But cosmic whispers dance inside.

I touch the soil, I feel the stone,
Yet sense that I am not alone.
The sky above, so vast, so wide,
A mirror to the fire inside.

For I am both, I walk betwixt,
A bridge of dust and light unfixed.
One part rooted, one part untamed,
A soul of stars—a child of waves.

Where the Wild Ones Roam

Beyond the maps, past marked-off lines,
Through tangled woods and gnarled vines,
Where rivers sing and mountains hum,
The wild ones wander—they call, they run.

No path is set, no cage, no chain,
They dance with thunder, kiss the rain.
Their hearts beat fierce, untamed, alive,
The pulse of earth, the soul's deep drive.

They chase the winds, they trust the tide,
With fearless steps, they walk, they glide.
For freedom lives in those who roam,
And every road can be a home.

Passports & Past Lives

A footstep falls on foreign ground,
Yet something stirs, so soft, profound.
A street I've walked, a name I know,
Though how or why—I cannot show.

The air is thick with déjà vu,
The echoes hum, the past shines through.
A stranger's glance, a voice, a song,
A feeling I have carried for so long.

Perhaps these stones recall my tread,
A piece of me was never dead.
For though my passport holds no trace,
My soul has always known this place.

The Map is in Your Bones

No compass points, no lines are drawn,
Yet something pulls me, leads me on.
A whisper deep, a quiet thread,
A voice that guides the road ahead.

The signs aren't written, clear and bright,
They flicker soft, like candlelight.
A fleeting dream, a tingle near,
A sudden pull that feels so clear.

Not all who wander lose their way,
Some hear the path in what won't stay.
For maps can fade, and stars can roam,
But what's within will lead you home.

Lost to Be Found

I wandered far, I lost my way,
The sky grew dark, the path went gray.
No signs, no maps, no guiding star,
Just endless roads that stretched too far.

But in the silence, soft and deep,
I found the truths I swore to keep.
Not in the plans I left behind,
But in the stillness of my mind.

For losing self is not the end,
But where the soul begins to mend.
So let me drift, let me roam,
For every step will bring me home.

Sacred Places, Sacred Lessons

The mountains teach me how to stand,
The rivers show what's out of hand.
The forests whisper, soft yet strong,
That roots can stretch but still belong.

The ocean sings of ebb and flow,
Of letting go, of all we know.
The deserts hum of quiet grace,
That empty space is still a place.

The roads I walk, the lands I see,
Are mirrors of the soul in me.
For every place, both far and near,
Holds lessons only I can hear.

Chasing Sunsets, Catching Dreams

I chase the sun as it slips low,
A golden fire, a crimson glow.
The sky ignites, then fades to blue,
A fleeting spark, yet something new.

For in that glow, so wild, so free,
I see the light inside of me.
A dream once dim now burns so bright,
Like fading sun turned into night.

Some say the day must end too fast,
That beauty fades, it doesn't last.
But every dusk and dawn agrees—
The light still lives inside of me.

So let me run, let me roam,
Find new skies to call my own.
For every step, each place I've been,
Is where the sun will rise again.

A Suitcase Full of Spells

I pack my bag, but light, not full,
No weight to bear, no heavy pull.
No fear, no doubt, no past regret,
Just dreams I haven't chased quite yet.

A charm for luck, a map of skies,
A whispered wish, a spark that flies.
A spell of trust, a thread of grace,
A heart that knows it owns its place.

No room for "what if," none for "stay,"
The road ahead won't wait all day.
So off I go, no backward glance,
Just open hands and wide-eyed chance.

For all I need is packed inside,
No extra weight, no need to hide.
A suitcase full of spells and air,
And faith to take me anywhere.

Wanderer's Blessing

May the road be kind, the skies be clear,
May every step dissolve your fear.
May doors swing wide where paths seem closed,
And whispers guide where no one knows.

May stars above reflect your light,
And moonbeams guard you through the night.
May rivers sing, may mountains stand tall,
To hold you strong in lands unknown to all.

May time bend soft, may winds stay true,
May every road lead back to you.
For where you go, you'll always find—
The magic walks close by your side.

Becoming

I was the seed beneath the stone,
Afraid to break, to stand alone.
Yet deep inside, the roots still grew,
A whisper soft, *you're meant for new*.

I was the bud with petals tight,
Too scared to reach, to chase the light.
Yet seasons turned, and so did I,
Unfolding wide beneath the sky.

I am the bloom, unbound, alive,
No longer yearning to arrive.
For all I sought was always near,
A voice within that said, *I'm here*.

I'll be the vine, the branch, the tree,
Forever growing, wild and free.

You Are the Key

I searched for signs in falling stars,
In tarot spreads and ancient scars.
In whispered words and echoed pasts,
But answers slipped, too fast, too vast.

I knocked on doors, I begged the night,
For fate to carve my path in light.
Yet every turn, each lock I tried,
Just led me back to where I'd cried.

The maps were false, the roads untrue,
For none could lead where I once knew.
And all along, beneath my plea,
The door was sealed inside of me.

Crowned by Fire

The flames arose, they took their claim,
They burned my past, they spoke my name.
I cried, I begged, I cursed the spark,
But fire does not fear the dark.

It licked my wounds, it stole my skin,
Unraveled all I'd buried in.
The walls I built, the lies I spun,
Turned into ash, undone, undone.

I swore I'd lost, that all was gone,
Yet in the smoke, I stood upon—
A throne of embers, fierce and bright,
A crown that dripped in molten light.

For fire never comes in vain,
It scorches doubt, it sears the chain.
And those who rise from flame and pyre,
Will rule the world, crowned by fire.

Unshackled

They wrapped me tight in ropes unseen,
In whispered doubt, in might-have-beens.
They told me, *stay, be small, be still,*
A bird with clipped and broken will.

I wore the chains, I played their part,
A heavy weight upon my heart.
Yet deep inside, a fire burned,
A quiet voice that cried, it's time to turn.

I pulled, I tore, I bled, I swayed,
The rusted locks began to fray.
The binds that once had shaped my fate,
Lay shattered now—too late, too late.

I stand, unbound, with breath anew,
No longer caged by what they knew.
For wings will grow where chains once fell,
And those who break will rise as well.

No Permission Needed

I do not ask, I do not wait,
For doors to swing or hands to shake.
No crown was placed upon my head—
I forged my throne, I broke, I bled.

They watch, they whisper, scoff, and sneer,
Yet none have walked these miles near.
Their rules, their lines, their careful pace—
I've burned them all without a trace.

Come test my fire, come try your hand,
Come see if I will break on land.
For tides may turn and winds may shift,
Still, I do not bow, I will not drift.

So let them judge, let them seethe,
Let them choke on what I breathe.
For I was never theirs to mold,
And I am braver now than bold.

Beware the Witch

They whispered once, they whisper still,
That witches bend the world with will.
That fire bows, that storms obey,
That fate itself is laced with clay.

Let them whisper—let them fear,
For I have burned and I am here.
No stake, no rope, no sharpened blade,
Can sever what the gods have made.

I stir the stars, I shape the tide,
I weave my spells, then I step aside.
For curses break where I have tread,
And ghosts still kneel before my stead.

So test me once, but not again,
For I am not the witch back when.
No torch, no stone, no priestly cries—
Can stop the storm that fills my eyes.

A Witch Goes Where She Pleases

I wake with the moon still kissing the sky,
With spells in my breath and stars in my eyes.
I walk through this world with the knowing of
old,
A whisper of fire, a heartbeat of gold.

The coffee stirs as if hearing my call,
The wind shifts first, then footsteps fall.
Candles flicker though no one is near,
I do not chase—I pull things here.

I do not beg, I do not wait,
The world bends soft beneath my fate.
I step, I claim, I turn, I weave,
What's meant for me will never leave.

They stare, they wonder, they shake their heads,
At magic stitched in words I've said.
But witches move how witches must—
By faith, by fire, by bone-deep trust.

Ancestral Echoes

Their whispers hum beneath my skin,
A chorus soft, yet fierce within.
I hear them stir the winds at night,
In flickered flame and silvered light.

Their battles carved into my bones,
Their spells still speak in undertones.
A thousand lives, a thousand names,
Yet all their fires burn the same.

I walk the path their feet once knew,
The roads they dreamed, I wander too.
Not lost, not lone, not cast astray—
They walk beside me day by day.

So let them watch, let doubt be near,
Let voices scoff, let silence sneer.
For I am forged from those long past—
And I will rise like they—steadfast.

The Soul Knows First

Before the signs, before the proof,
Before the path reveals its truth,
A whisper stirs, a feeling calls,
An unseen hand that breaks the walls.

The mind may doubt, the heart may shake,
But deep within, no step's mistake.
For fate is not a thing we chase,
It makes the hour, it sets the pace.

A shiver, pause, a shift in air,
A knowing glance, a quiet stare.
The body hums, the spirit sighs,
The truth was there before the eyes.

So heed the pull, embrace the glow,
The mind asks how, the soul says go.

The Signs Were Always There

The feather fell, the clock struck true,
The same three numbers came in view.
A flickered light, a whispered name,
A song that played and felt the same.

I called for signs, I begged to see,
For fate to leave a clue for me.
Yet looking back, they stood in sight,
Like stars that pierced against the night.

Not flashing bright, not bold and loud,
But woven soft within the shroud.
For those who watch, for those who care,
The signs were always, always there.

A Love Note from the Universe

You are not lost, you've never strayed,
The stars still know the wish you made.
The wind still sings your quiet name,
The tides still turn, the sparks remain.

You ask for signs, for proof, for fate,
But love has never come too late.
The path you walk, the steps you take,
Are shaping dreams you've yet to wake.

So hush, be still, release the fear,
The things you seek are drawing near.
For every wish cast to the sky,
Comes back in time—just trust, just try.

The Path That Calls

A road unmarked, a trail unknown,
A whispered pull that feels like home.
No map in hand, no guiding sign,
Yet still, I walk—the path is mine.

The world may scoff, may shake its head,
"Stay safe," they warn, "Choose known instead."
But hearts don't race for paved, sure ground,
They long for lands yet to be found.

The wind will shift, the light may fade,
Yet forward steps will still be made.
For even lost, my soul can see—
The way ahead was made for me.

So let me go, let me roam,
Let me chase the stars alone.
For even lost, I'm never wrong—
The path that calls has called me long.

Stars in My Pocket

I keep a wish inside my hand,
A secret spark, a grain of sand.
A dream too big, a light too wild,
Yet cradled soft—my inner child.

I fold the sky, I tuck it tight,
A pocket full of quiet light.
No storm can steal, no night erase,
The glow I carry from place to place.

For dreams aren't lost, they do not fade,
They hum within, they hold, they wait.
And every time I reach inside,
I find the stars still burn alive.

The Frequency of Abundance

Abundance hums, it sings, it sways,
It flows in endless, golden waves.
Not chased, not forced, not held too tight,
But drawn to those who shine just right.

It is not luck, it is not rare,
It moves where hearts and hands prepare.
It answers joy, it answers trust,
It multiplies where love is just.

A current deep, unseen yet near,
It bends to those who have no fear.
For wealth is not in what we keep,
But what we give and what we speak.

Your Name is Written in the Stars

The night is vast, the sky so wide,
Yet still, it knows what burns inside.
A fate once whispered, soft yet strong,
A story waiting all along.

No wish is lost, no dream too far,
Your name is written in the stars.
The cosmos hums, the planets turn,
For all you seek, the stars have learned.

So walk with trust, let doubt release,
The universe moves piece by piece.
And even when you cannot see,
The stars still shine—they wait for thee.

For threads unseen still weave and spin,
The signs, the doors, all pull you in.
No path is wrong, no time is late,
What's meant for you will hold and wait.

Alchemy of Thought

A thought is small, a fleeting spark,
A whisper dancing in the dark.
Yet tend it well, yet shape it true,
And watch what dreams are born anew.

For words have weight, and thoughts can mold,
They turn to silver, shift to gold.
They pull, they weave, they twist, they spin,
The world reflects what grows within.

So mind the tales you tell, you claim,
For every fear can call its name.
But those who dream, who dare, who trust,
Will watch their world rise up from dust.

The Soul Knows First

Before the mind can trace the way,
Before the heart dares hope or stay,
A whisper stirs, a tug, a spark,
A knowing deep within the dark.

The body hums, the breath stands still,
A silent nudge, a quiet thrill.
No map in hand, no proof, no guide,
Yet something beckons from inside.

The mind may fight, the doubt may rise,
Yet fate still flickers in the eyes.
For those who trust, who heed, who go,
Will find the soul had known it so.

Not left to chance, nor tossed by fate,
Each step aligns, though some seem late.
The path unfolds in perfect time,
Each turn, each sign—a cosmic rhyme.

Magnetism

I do not chase, I do not plead,
What's meant for me is drawn with speed.
Not by force and not by fight,
But by the way I shine my light.

I tune my heart, I set my gaze,
And watch the world shift in my place.
For what I seek is seeking too,
A dance of fate, a thread pulled through.

No grasping hands, no fear, no lack,
The tides flow forth, then circle back.
For all I am and all I'll be,
Becomes the force that comes to me.

Whispers from the Wind

The wind will hum, the leaves will dance,
The world will speak if given chance.
A feather falls, a shadow bends,
A message sent, though none intend.

A hush, a pause, a shifting air,
A sign arrives from who-knows-where.
Not bold, not loud, yet still it stays,
A whisper threading through my days.

For those who watch, for those who hear,
The quiet voice is always near.
No words, no script, yet clear as flame—
The wind still knows and calls my name.

The Present is the Portal

Not in the past, nor in the plan,
Not in the "someday" close at hand.
Not in the wishing, nor in delay,
But only here, only today.

The breath I take, the step I tread,
The thoughts that spiral inside my head.
Each fleeting moment, soft yet bright,
A key that turns, a spark of light.

The doors I chase, the fate I crave,
Are not beyond, they are not saved.
For all I seek, both vast and small,
Exists within this moment's call.

So let me wake, so let me see,
The power lives inside of me.
No need to wait, no need to run,
The magic's here—it's just begun.

The Quiet Between

The steps are taken, the seeds are sown,
The fate I've shaped is not my own.
And now I wait in hollow air,
Where doubt and fear begin to flare.

What if I've failed? What if I've lost?
What if the path will count the cost?
My mind constructs walls of worst-case fate,
A prison built by those who wait.

Yet nothing shifts, no doors swing wide,
No voice confirms I've turned the tide.
So all I do is stand and see—
If all I've done was meant to be.

Breath Magic

A breath drawn deep, a whispered name,
A spark within, a tempered flame.
Inhale hope and exhale doubt,
Let silence chase the worry out.

The rise, the fall, the measured flow,
A rhythm ancient souls still know.
No need for words, no plea, no prayer,
The magic stirs within the air.

So breathe in strong, so breathe in slow,
Let tides within their courses go.
For spells aren't cast with smoke alone,
But in the breath we call our own.

Lessons in a Sunrise

The sky does not demand the light,
Nor beg the sun to end the night.
It waits in hush, it waits in trust,
It knows the dawn will come as must.

No rush, no force, no frantic plea,
Just certainty the glow will be.
No clock, no hand, yet still it climbs,
A lesson carved in silent time.

Some things can't bend, some doors won't shake,
Some tides will rise when meant to wake.
For even shadows, long and deep,
Will bow before the light they keep.

So let me learn, so let me rest,
And trust that I have done my best.
For just like the light returns once more,
What's meant for me will reach my door.

The Magic of Doing Nothing

A spell is cast in word and deed,
In fire bright and planted seed.
Yet magic bends to will alone—
And sometimes, stillness stands its own.

I shape the world with hands and mind,
Yet not all doors are mine to find.
Not every battle needs my sword,
Not every game must see me score.

To stand, to breathe, to let things lie,
Is not to lose, but to decide.
For those who build their fate with care,
Know when to act—and when to spare.

Holding Space for Yourself

I have been open, wide and true,
A place where others ran straight through.
I've been the light, the open door,
A place of rest—a steady shore.

But now I stand, both fierce and free,
A home, a haven just for me.
No walls too high, no locks in place,
Yet only love may share this space.

I give myself the room to grow,
To heal, to breathe, to simply know.
For those who build a world within,
Will never feel alone again.

The Art of Surrender

I held too tight, I fought the tide,
I clenched my fists, refused to glide.
Yet water moves where hands let go,
And trust is taught in ebb, in flow.

I chased, I begged, I swore, I cried,
Demanded fate stand by my side.
But stars don't shine from caged commands,
They burn for those with open hands.

I feared the pause, the space, the wait,
As if the stars could lose my fate.
Yet time unfolds in ways unknown,
And all arrives in space my own..

So here I stand, unbound, unchained,
No need to force, no will restrained.
For what is mine will find its way,
No need to fight—I let it stay.

Grounded and Galactic

I walk with roots beneath my feet,
The steady pulse, the earthen beat.
Yet stars still hum within my veins,
A universe I can't explain.

I plant, I build, I stitch, I weave,
Yet drift where cosmic dreamers leave.
A heart in soil, a head in space,
A life that bends yet knows its place.

I speak with trees, I read the sky,
I taste the wind as worlds pass by.
A being shaped from dust and sun,
Both made and maker, both in one.

I am the dust, I am the sky,
The rooted ground, the reason why.
A force unseen, a spark so bright,
Both here, both vast—both dark and light.

The Soul's True Home

I searched through lands both vast and wide,
Through mountain peaks and oceans' tide.
Each place I stood, I wished to stay,
Yet something called me far away.

I traced the stars, I read the signs,
I walked through lifetimes, past and mine.
I swore that home was where I'd been,
Yet home was never bound by skin.

No walls, no doors, no anchored keep,
No soil to claim, no roots too deep.
For home is not where maps convey,
But where the heart dares carve its way.

So let me roam, let me be free,
Let restless winds still carry me.
For those who walk with open hands,
Find home in all, yet need no lands.

A Universe in Bloom

The stars are seeds, the sky a field,
A cosmos spun, a dream revealed.
A garden vast, still stretching wide,
With roots unseen, through time unplied.

The sun it grows, the void it breathes,
A bloom of worlds beyond belief.
Each thought, each spark, each whispered tune,
A petal soft, a fate in bloom.

For galaxies are born in hands,
In hearts that dare, in minds that dance.
And every wish, both wild and new,
Becomes a bud—a world in view.

So let me bloom, so let me rise,
Expand like dusk, like painted skies.
For I am more than dust and bone—
A universe forever grown.

The Ache of Almost

I almost touched it, almost knew,
A fleeting spark, a glimpse of blue.
The door was there, the path was laid,
Yet somehow, still, I lost my way.

A whisper left upon my skin,
A love that burned but stayed within.
A fate so close, a breath, a thread,
A word unspoken, left for dead.

Not lost, not found, just in between,
A ghost of what I've never seen.
The weight of all I'll never hold,
Yet somehow still, it feels like gold.

So let me ache, let me regret,
Let me mourn what never met.
For even dreams that slip and fade,
Can haunt the heart like love once made.

The Knife You Left

You swore your hands were soft, were kind,
Yet carved your name along my spine.
Not with steel, not with a blade,
But every vow you ever betrayed.

You smiled as if the wound was light,
As if the blade had slipped just right.
And maybe, once, I called it love,
Before I saw the blood run rough.

The wound has closed, the scar remains,
A mark that time cannot explain.
For even healed, the heart still knows,
The knife you left was yours to hold.

So take it back, go claim your sin,
I am not yours to cut again.
For blades may pierce and wounds may stay,
But even steel will rust away.

The Hands That Never Trembled

I braced for storms, for raging tides,
For love that burned, then bled, then died.
I learned to flinch before the fall,
To build my walls, to trust them tall.

But then you came, with steady hands,
No rush, no weight, no harsh demands.
You did not fix, you did not mend,
Yet still, I learned to breathe again.

No promises, no perfect lines,
No need to claim what once was mine.
You only stayed, you only cared,
And somehow, that was love laid bare.

For love is not a grand display,
Not words that beg, not games we play.
It's hands that never trembled near,
It's kindness, quiet, pulling near.

The Mirror Was a Lie

You held a mirror to my face,
Said, Look at you—so out of place.
Each flaw, each crack, you traced so well,
You turned my mind into a cell.

You pulled the strings, you wrote the lines,
Yet swore the fault was only mine.
And every time I tried to flee,
You whispered, *Who would love but me?*

I bent, I shrank, I tried to change,
I played the part, I took the blame.
Yet even small, you raged, you swore—
How dare I not make space for more?

But now I see, the glass was bent,
A funhouse trick, a false lament.
The flaws you swore were mine alone—
Were cracks within yourself unknown.

The Game You Played

You moved the line, you changed the rules,
Then laughed at me for playing the fool.
You swore I lost, you swore I strayed,
Yet it was I who'd been betrayed.

You pulled the thread, then blamed the fray,
You lit the match, then ran away.
You swore I screamed too loud, too much,
And flinched away at every clutch.

You stacked the deck, then called me mad,
For folding hands you swore I had.
You dealt the lies, you skewed the facts,
Then gasped when I stopped coming back.

You built the fire, then cursed my name,
For dancing barefoot in the flames.
You swore I shattered, broke, betrayed—
But I just quit the game you played.

Rebuilt in My Own Name

You left me in ruins, dust and bone,
A life once claimed but never owned.
You swore I'd break, you swore I'd fade,
Yet here I stand—rebuilt, remade.

No borrowed light, no stolen throne,
No name but that which I have sown.
No hands but mine, no will, no claim,
No voice to shape me by their name.

I rose, I walked, I burned, I grew,
No longer shaped by love untrue.
I left the ashes where they lay—
And rose in fire, my sovereign way.

And now you watch, and now you see,
The power you once feared in me.
For I am here, I've staked my claim—
Rebuilt in fire, reborn in name.

Grateful for the Storm

The winds once howled, the skies once tore,
Was sure I'd drowned, no sight of shore.
Yet now I stand, the tempest passed,
All I lost was never meant to last.

The rain it carved, the winds they wailed,
They shattered walls I thought prevailed.
Yet in the wreckage, torn and tossed,
I found the self I thought was lost.

For storms don't come to take, but show,
The things that must be stripped to grow.
And now I see, through past so worn—
I was not lost. I was reborn.

So let it rage, so let it pour,
I fear the breaking winds no more.
For every storm that left me bare,
Made room for light beyond compare.

For the Ones Who Stayed

Not all who love will stand the test,
Some leave when skies are dark at best.
But some remain, through flood and flame,
Their hands unchanged, their hearts the same.

They saw me break, they watched me bend,
Yet never doubted I would mend.
No whispered shame, no turning back,
Just quiet love where I once lacked.

They did not fix, they did not save,
Yet still, they held me through the waves.
And in their presence, strong and true,
I found the strength to pull me through.

So here's my vow, here's my grace,
To cherish love that won't change face.
For in a world that shifts like sand,
Some hearts remain—and those still stand.

For Every Version of Me

To the one who stayed when they let go,
Who held her ground through every low.
Who swallowed pain with quiet grace,
Yet never let it steal her place.

To the one who fought when all seemed lost,
Who paid the price, who knew the cost.
Who walked through fire, through ache, through war,
Yet never asked for something more.

To the one who cried but still stood tall,
Who stitched herself from every fall.
Who swore that one day, she would see—
A life beyond the misery.

For every version, bruised yet free,
Who paved the road that led to me—
I stand today, unbowed, unbent,
A testament to what they meant.

Where Fate has Led

To the whisper low, the pull so slight,
The spark that glows in silent night.
To every sign, to every thread,
To paths unseen where fate has led.

To every "no" that saved my soul,
To every loss that made me whole.
To doors that locked, to roads that veered,
Yet still, I somehow ended here.

To hands I've never seen, yet feel,
To wounds once deep that learned to heal.
To all the light I could not see—
Yet still, it never lost sight of me.

So here I stand, both fierce and free,
Forever held by what must be.
For all I've sought, for all I'll see—
The magic always moves through me.

And So It Is

I stand complete, I need not chase,
What's meant for me finds sacred space.
No force required, no chains to bind,
For what is mine was always mine.

I do not fear what comes, what stays,
The tides will turn in their own ways.
And when they do, I stand, I trust,
For all unfolds as all things must.

No dream too big, no fate too far,
No wish too wild to reach the stars.
The path, the spark, the pull, the guide—
Were always burning bright inside.

So here I stand, so here I stay,
No more to lose, no debts to pay.
I ask, I claim, I trust, I know—
And so it is. And so it flows.

www.ingramcontent.com/pod-product-compliance
Lightning Source LLC
La Vergne TN
LVHW011053200726
843509LV00011B/1393